Table Of Contents

Chapter 1: What Is Stand-Up Comedy?

Stand-Up Comedy: An Overview

Stand-up comedy is a profession devoted to the pursuit of humor. That said, it is a solitary endeavor: stand-up comedians perform alone before a crowd. While all stand-up comedians have their own type of humor, their own opinions about what is or is not funny, and their own strange idiosyncrasies, they all have two things in common: they fly solo and they *like to make people laugh*. The first and most important requirement for entering this grueling profession as a full-time performer — being paid to tell jokes and stories to a live audience — is to be funny.

There are many different types of comedy: from the improvisational acts found on shows like "Whose Line Is It Anyway?" to the comedy clubs specializing in stand-up. The latter is especially flexible and can include anything from **character comedy**, like impersonations and imitations, to **slapstick comedy**, like over-the-top displays that exceed the boundaries of common sense. There's physical comedy, black comedy, blue comedy, and even surreal comedy, which plays on absurdism and juxtaposition. Stand-up comics throughout history have utilized all these forms of humor and continue to do so today.

Sketches, sitcoms, improv troupes, spoofs, and satires are examples of other forms of comedic entertainment from outside the stand-up realm. They all involve multiple performers and focus more on storytelling. While the most successful stand-up comics often cross over into other forms of comedy, the stand-up realm focuses on the consistent and quick delivery of humorous one-liners, longer jokes, or anecdotes that comprise a monologue. Stand-up comedy is about making people laugh *right away*.

Stand-up comedy requires open communication with an audience. The act is fun for neither the comic nor the audience if no one's laughing. The stand-up comic's job is, simply put, to stream a constant stream of hilarity out of his or her mouth until the audience members' stomachs are sore from laughing. (And, of course, *full* after imbibing the required two drink minimum at most comedy clubs). But just as stand-up isn't the only form of comedy out there, being funny isn't the only requirement for becoming a stand-up comedian.

Chapter 2: Careers In Comedy

Comedy Careers

I used to play in bands. I had to rely on three other dudes with drug problems and girlfriend problems. Doing improv involves relying on a group of people, on other people being funny. I don't like to rely on other people. The greatest thing about stand-up is that whether you fail or succeed is completely up to you and does not depend on anybody else. Not to mention, it's more lucrative when you're just one person. You don't have to split the income with anyone else. You go to New York, there are probably two places where you can see improv, and 15 major comedy clubs.

Most people have to have other careers, especially when they're just getting started with stand-up. You can't just decide you want to be a stand-up comedian and start making money tomorrow. It isn't a lucrative living, and you have to work for years to make any living at all. Treat it as a hobby in the beginning and have another job until you are confident you can support yourself as a stand-up comedian.

Before television and radio, comics could spend years perfecting a single act. Stand-up comedy originated in British music halls in the late 19th century, where comedians' acts were subject to censorship. They were forced to read exactly what they had planned after submitting their monologues to the chamberlain for editing.

Television and radio changed everything, increasing demand for material and getting rid of scripting and censorship requirements. Careers in comedy became more attractive. Today the most successful comedians can write for television and radio, make podcasts, have their own talk shows, and put their work on YouTube. But stand-up still remains one of the most respected forms of comedy.

Stand-up is a solo act: the comedian must depend only on him or herself. Of course, there's a big group of people in the audience who have to think you're funny, but the stand-up comedian is the sole writer and editor of material. They are the performer, producer, promoter, and technician all in one. The reward that comes from developing a rapport with the audience and keeping them laughing through an entire act is priceless.

When it comes to stand-up, there isn't as much structural pressure as there is in the production of a television show or a theatrical play. Stand-up is about getting *immediate laughs*. That being said, the best stand-up comedians are fully versed in the art of storytelling, and understand how to set up a story arc within a series of jokes, even if the audience isn't following specific plot. Stand-up is perfect for perfectionists: the best stand-up acts have been nursed and cared for — edited and re-edited over time — and constantly groomed until they are perfect.

While stand-up comedy may be demanding as an art form, it's also very malleable. It can be a hobby or a full-time job, and it's an avenue into other, more corporate careers. Many public speakers trained in stand-up comedy can make up to $25,000 per speech, and they aren't even famous. They are simply well trained, articulate speakers who started as aspiring stand-up comedians.

Chapter 3: Breaking Into Stand-Up Comedy

The 12 Best Tips For Breaking Into Stand-Up Comedy

1. Educate Yourself.

Going to as many comedy shows as you can, whether they be open mic nights, free local shows, or comedy shows at bigger, more established comedy clubs, is the first step to becoming a full-time stand-up comedian. There is no comedian you admire that didn't start out in the audience. Follow comedians you admire. Twitter, Facebook, and YouTube are great places to educate yourself about your favorite comedians. Twitter — home to one-line witticisms — is a haven for budding comedians and experienced comedians alike. Follow your favorites on Twitter to see what they're talking about and what new material they are releasing, as well as what websites they follow and which fellow comedians *they* admire. Whenever you're in a new city, check out the comedy shows or clubs nearby. Absorb different forms of cultural humor whenever you can, and see what other people think is funny. If nothing else, you'll learn something.

2. Take A Public Speaking Class.

Comedy is just a form of public speaking. To think outside the box, join your local Toastmasters International group for helpful tips on public speaking, and another community or people who could help forward your career. Visit http://www.toastmasters.org/ for details.

3. Take A Comedy Class.

Jerry Seinfeld once said "Comedy is the hardest thing you can do. If you can do that you can do anything." Before I was a stand-up comedian, I was working as a senior engineer at Intel. My job was to travel around the world with the co-founder and design technical demonstrations to present on stage with them. The technical part is something I can do in my sleep – being Indian and Japanese helps – but the tough part was speaking on stage in front of thousands of people, sometimes millions on television. It was really, really terrifying to speak in front of people so I thought I'd take a public speaking class to get over my stage fright. I joined the Intel Toastmasters club on campus. Although that helped a little bit, being in front of 12 other geeks at lunchtime just couldn't stimulate being in front of thousands of people. Taking a comedy class would scratch my urge to try to break into comedy and have the benefit of easing my fear of speaking on stage.

You probably won't just be good at something you haven't tried. Take a class and learn from the experts. Comedy classes are positive environments and places to build community that will teach you a lot of things about comedy that the naked eye can't see at first glance. Judy Carter in Los Angeles and Steve Rosenfield at the American Comedy Institute in New York are two very well-respected teachers to consider. You can also check out The Groundlings, Upright Citizens Brigade, local 4 year universities that offer extension classes, open classes at your local community college, and local improv or sketch comedy groups in your area to find comedy classes near you.

4. Go To Open Mic Nights.

The motto for open mic nights is "grind it out." Come up with 5 minutes of stuff — anything you can — and go brave the hecklers, small crowds, and other cynical comedians. Some may call it psychologically destructive; but you've got to get experience somewhere. Learning to develop your act, not to mention a thick skin, is invaluable.

Don't get scared away, no matter how humiliating the open mic might be.Open mics may be a really terrifying way to get started; but they are also a necessary way to get your foot in the door. Jerry Seinfeld said in an interview that he was afraid of comedy for years, and yet now he's a famous comedian. Procrastination is a common thread among many comedians, who thought about breaking into comedy for years and now have tremendous regret that they did not start sooner. Don't put it off. Get over the fear. There's a great saying: do what you fear and the death of fear is certain.

5. Network, Network, Network.

Talk to booking managers and club owners after shows. Talk to other comedians you know or admire. Talk to teachers and fellow classmates and involve yourself in whatever community you can find. Talk to whoever will listen, listen to whoever will talk, and exchange contact information whenever you can. If you're traveling, talk to the person next to you on a plane. Stand at the back of the comedy club after you perform. Sell CDs and give out business cards to anyone who will accept them.

6. WRITE, WRITE, WRITE.

I met a comedian when I was managing at Intel and asked him how he got into the business. He said "Listen, when you hear something that's funny or say something funny just write it down, otherwise you'll forget it."

Don't stop writing. Write down anything and everything you think is funny before you forget it. Keep a brainstorming notebook on you, or use your phone to keep a running list of jokes. That way when you sit down to give yourself writing time, you won't be starting from scratch. If you keep writing over the course of six months, you may come up with a potential hour of comedy. That's enough to be turned into an act.

7. Take Advantage of the Internet.

I think nowadays it goes without saying that you need a basic technological sense. I run into so many comedians who are magnificent, but don't have business cards or websites. There's a guy in DC who is one of the funniest comedians I've ever seen. But I can't find him. He's got a really generic name: Dave George. How do you find this guy? He doesn't have a website or a business card, and I can't believe I'm the only person who'd like to get a hold of him. A booker in DC recently sent out a list of 30 comedians to America's Got Talent. I was on the list and they're looking at me now, probably because 10 of those comedians didn't have websites. Those technical skills are just tools that you need to have in this day and age.

Put yourself out there. Upload videos, start a blog, tweet your jokes, email your friends. Face to face meetings are hard to come by, but the Internet is a place where everyone can get exposure.

8. Stop worrying what other people think.

A friend of mine wrote a book called <u>100 Ways to Motivate Yourself</u>*. He argues that when we're children, we're full of dreams and visions, idealistic and open to things. "I want to be a race car driver" or "I want to be a basketball player." Sometime around high school or college, reality sets in. We give up our dreams and try to conform to what everyone else is doing. A lot of my time is spent on the road. I eat alone in restaurants frequently, and I think there's a kind of stigma to that. People are afraid to do that. When the maitre'd yells out "Table for one!" you can't be worried about what other people in that restaurant think of you.*

Get out of the mold of caring what other people think, especially when you're off stage. Don't worry about skepticism. Don't distract yourself with destructive thoughts about whether or not you're going to fail. Be resilient. To be a successful comedian, you have to have a very thick skin.

9. Develop a good business sense.

I meet comedians all the time who will get calls from companies saying "Hey, I saw you at this comedy club, I'd like to book you for a corporate business event. What do you charge?" And they'll respond "200 bucks." Who knows? That company might have been willing to pay you $10,000.

Learn how to write a contract. The information is available online. You can look it up. Wake up early and work when others aren't working. There are so many comedians who want to be stars, but they get up at 5pm. Meanwhile, all the auditions for movies and television are going on during the business day. You have to have a business mentality, a business state of mind. So many great comedians don't have this rudimentary business knowledge and it hurts them.

10. Be industrious.

I often hear "Oh I'm on the road, I'm in the condo, there are 6 hours before the show. I'm bored. I have nothing to do."

Constantly be working. Focus on marketing yourself and your business. Every second of every day is something. You can be working on your website, writing new jokes, practicing your jokes, editing jokes, making podcasts, editing your videos, etc. You must have a work ethic and be willing to put in the hours. It's not just about waking up at 6pm, doing the show at 8pm, and then partying all night.

11. Stay away from substance abuse.

I don't drink at all, but I see it everywhere among comedians in New York. I see guys who do drink, who I haven't seen in two years. They look like they've aged ten.

Stay away from the self-destructive stuff. Especially drugs and alcohol. There's nothing wrong with having a drink, but so many comedians can't get on stage without being stoned or drunk. Comedy is an industry filled with self destructive behavior. But so many comedians get signed to huge management companies and then get dropped because they can't stay on the wagon.

12. Don't Get Discouraged.

On the one hand, you may never really feel like you've made it. There are probably people who are much more well known and famous than you are. But when you get to a point where you can make your living, that's a big milestone. And the milestones only get bigger and bigger as you progress.

Stand-up comedy is brutal. Audiences expect a lot from the folks on stage. What's more, many aspiring comedians are fighting for the same spots at comedy clubs, festivals and open mic nights. There's no greater humiliation than being up on stage — especially when you're starting out — and not knowing how to act. But as a beginner, letting yourself get thrown off as a result performance anxiety can completely derail your career.

If you have a Friday or Saturday night off, don't be self-conscious that you're at home working while other people are out. That's something to be proud of. Keep your head above water, don't get caught up in competition, and focus on your craft.

Chapter 4: Getting Started

www.hyperink.com   13

Make Your First Career Moves

I agonized for months before deciding to take my first comedy class. I drove 50 miles to San Francisco every week. The first class was an introduction. The second class: I brought all these jokes I'd been writing for years. I came in with this thick stack of mini index cards and the teacher said "whoa, you've got so many jokes I'm impressed." People laughed at every joke I read. This was a class of fifteen people, maybe twenty. If you're getting a few laughs from 15 people and you multiply that to 300 people in a club. It's exponential, the more people, the more laughs. The second performance, third class, nobody laughed at anything. I didn't know why; I couldn't figure out why. I was devastated. I thought I'd bombed; I came within a hair's breath of quitting. And now, it's terrifying to think about how different my life would have been if I'd quit.

I summoned the courage to tell myself this was one thing I didn't want to quit. It came time for the final exam, which was a performance. They rented out a comedy club and all my friends and relatives were invited. That's terrifying — makes you not want to invite anybody in case you bomb. We were all terrified. The one thing I decided to do was to be really prepared, to know my act backwards and forwards. I'd go to the gym and recite it to myself in my head. On the day of the show I rented a conference room at Intel and said it over and over. I read it to my girlfriend of the time on the phone. She laughed at some but not all of it, which was disconcerting. I knew those six minutes word for word. I invited three friends. The place was packed. I noticed I couldn't see a thing — nothing but the people in front. That's terrifying. I went into my first joke and they just laughed and laughed at every single joke, except for one. Which they didn't get. It was the most incredible experience I've ever had.

My first show went really well. I had a bit of an unusual situation because the second show just happened. I happened to have my tape with me at this comedy show in Las Vegas. I also happened to be with one of my friends at Intel doing booth duty, setting up the system for a big convention. So I mentioned to one of the guys that I'd just taken a comedy class that was awesome. He said "Let's see the tape." I showed him and he asked me if I'd like to perform at the team dinner that night on top of the hotel.

There were about 250 Intel people there. I did impressions of the chairman, Andy Grove, and some of the presidents. No comedian gets to perform in front of 200 people at a second show. Then one of the guys asked me if I could perform at the annual sales conference two months later. I said "Sure. How many people are going to be there?" and he said "about 2,500 people from around the world." Every country sends their best sales reps to this conference. I never actually told my boss about it because I thought he'd say no.

I rehearsed the day before and all of the senior executives at Intel were at the rehearsal. I rehearsed the whole act including one of my impressions of Bill Clinton. They were just laughing and laughing and laughing. So that proved my act was okay. The next day I perform. It was a Monday morning, eight o'clock. Nobody had been drinking. To open up the convention we pretended that something had gone wrong with one of my demos. I said "Hey, I'm Dan Nainan, one of my computers died. Something's gone wrong, so while we're waiting to fix that I'm gonna tell you some jokes." My left leg was literally shaking I was so terrified.

They loved my impression of Andy Grove. He's like the Steve Jobs of Intel, with a thick Hungarian accent. A headstrong, abrupt type of guy. He'll turn to someone in a meeting who hasn't said anything and he'll say "How do you add value to this meeting?" He's one of the founders of Intel, a great man, but very intimidating. Here I am, a new comedian, it's my third show ever, and I just kill it. Afterwards all these people who didn't know me came up afterwards and said "You aren't really an Intel demo guy, right? You're a professional comedian?" and I said "No I'm actually an Intel demo guy." That was when I got the first inkling that I could do this for a living.

Following the **12 Best Tips in Chapter Three** will help you break into the stand-up comedy world. But everyone has a different timeline for success. Create your own timeline and set realistic goals for yourself along the way.

Reward yourself for reaching milestones like getting a certain number of followers on Twitter, putting up YouTube videos, or booking gigs. Remember: full-time stand-up comedians often work extremely long days, especially comedians who have branched out into writing for TV or other avenues outside of the stand-up world. Make sure to put a couple of hours (at a minimum) into your work each day in order to accomplish your goals.

For example, start taking a comedy class and make yourself go on stage a certain amount. After all, your success is dictated by one thing: how much you can get on stage. How good you will become is only a matter of practice.

Jerry Seinfeld once said that the number of years you've been doing stand-up is how old you are. Comedy is a highly iterative process. It's about constantly trying new jokes and then eliminating those that don't work. The longer you've been doing comedy, the more jokes you'll have. Five years of work makes you barely literate in comparison to veteran stand-up comedians like Bill Cosby, Whoopi Goldberg, and Robin Williams. Want to see results faster than that? Put in more hours. The more dedicated you become, the funnier you'll be — and the more shows you'll book.

Participating in "bringer shows", where you are allowed on stage if you bring more than ten people, is a great way to increase your stage experience. Bring you friends to boost your own confidence with laughs. Then, when you do really well at a comedy show, you'll have friends to say, "you know, I'm not just saying this but you were great." And at the very least, if you bomb, they'll be there to console you later — reminding you that, "you know, it takes a lot of guts to get up there all by yourself."

Chapter 5: Just The Jokes

Writing Your Material

Anything and everything gives me material for jokes. There's a bit of a filter I have to put on my writing. Just like any male comedian, I think of a lot of great dirty jokes. But unlike other comedians I can't do that material in my act. I have to prune. I'll write down dirty jokes and give them to other friends — but I don't use them.

I'm always seeing, hearing, and observing things that are funny. People tell me my stuff is intelligent humor. I didn't really believe that until I realized that stupid people don't get my jokes. I think about things like the UPS tracking number. Why does a number have to be that long? Because there haven't been that many packages in the history of man. I like absurdities, questioning why things are the way they are. It's a lot of stuff that just pops into my head — thoughts everybody has.

Some comedians write for eight hours a day. I don't have the focus for that. There are two types of writing: writing it down as it happens, and writing jokes for four hours straight. I stick to the former. My writing process is very spur of the moment. The type of stuff spans the spectrum.

Very early in my career I was doing a show at Gotham comedy club and there was a rumor that Jerry Seinfeld was going to show up to practice for his upcoming gig on Letterman. Whenever a comedian is getting ready to go on national TV they'll come to clubs to practice their act. And of course, if Jerry Seinfeld walks into a club and says "Hey! Can I do some time?" they'll put him up right away.

Sure enough he shows up in the lobby and said "Oh my god that's Jerry Seinfeld" and I went up to talk to him, even though people discourage that sort of thing. I said "Excuse me, Jerry (because I hate when people call me Mr. Nainan), I just started as a comedian and I'm curious if you have any advice for a beginning comedian." He was really nice. He said "you should work clean. You will work everywhere." I took that advice, and ever since then I've never put a single swear word in my comedy.

If you look at the shows I do now, almost every single one could not have a comedian who uses profanity, sexual vulgarity, or anything like that. That's actually my biggest selling point. It's a business decision, if nothing else. Plus vulgarity doesn't fit my persona. I don't think I could pull it off.

I did a show at the World Bank for 50-102 year old retirees. The next week I did a show in Boston for this private school for boys from 7th to 9th grade. So many comedians could never do shows like that. I don't want to do anything dirty and have my parents hear about it because they'd kill me. They're Asian and very conservative. Doing dirty jokes in front of my Indian Dad and Japanese Mom? That would not work.

Knowing yourself well will help you create the best material. Think about where you're from, what your family is like, how you were brought up and what was unique or humorous about that experience. Know what *you* think is funny before you start trying to please others.

Then think about how you relate to other people. What makes your friends laugh? What are the idiosyncrasies they love about you? Every detail helps the audience identify with you, so let them know who you are up front.

Comedians are often self-deprecating. It's part of the hilarity. To be a stand up comedian, you've got to have an inward-looking sense of humor. So know yourself, stick with what you know, and don't be afraid to laugh about it.

There's an established formula to comedy that will help you get started. A good act might look as follows: tell the audience about yourself and open with a very strong joke to capture the crowd's attention **immediately**. Then, toss out a few **feelers**. These are your B-level jokes: the second best level of material. See what makes them laugh, calculate how much you can get away with. Follow the feelers with some **builders**: low-key, casual jokes that you can execute well. These are the "**back pocket jokes**" that help you build up your routine.

Next, try out your **new material**. This is your C-level material: your weakest material, the new jokes you are trying. Interspersing new material with builders is also a great way to test the proverbial waters without letting the audience down. Then go for the A-level stuff. This is your **best material** – the funniest jokes you've got. The ones you've practiced over and over. The ones that work.

The jokes that work should be easily discernible from the jokes that don't: they get the loudest and longest laughs — and hopefully applause. Your best jokes should go at the end of the act, leaving the audience with a grand finale. Say thank you, stay confident, take a bow, and enjoy your applause.

Before you perform again, revisit your act and prune away the jokes that didn't get big laughs. Eventually you'll have a set that's guaranteed to make the crowd laugh.

In the meantime, here are a few tips to help you get started with your writing:

1. Exploit the entertainment that already exists in everyday life.

Get creative and look at every situation until you find the comedy in it. Observe the world around you and point out its absurdities. Read the newspaper, reflect on your personal relationships, remember what makes you connect with other people. This will help you relate to your audience.

2. Imitate others who make you laugh.

You don't need to be mean to be funny. But perfecting voices and gestures of other funny people is a great way to expand your repertoire.

3. Structure your jokes well.

Set up the situation. Prepare the audience for the punch line before you deliver it. Think about your word choice. Keep your punch lines short, sweet, and to the point.

4. Take notes.

Jot down a list of jokes and keep it in your back pocket in case you freeze up on stage. Drew Carey once said that for every ten jokes you write, one will be funny, so don't leave yourself with a shortage of material. Real time writing will help you accumulate this material. If you think of something that makes you laugh out loud in the shower, write it down. Who knows? You might make 3,000 other people laugh later. It might become one of your signature, back pocket jokes.

If you don't write it down, you risk losing it forever.

5. Keep it classy.

Social commentary is one thing. But avoid racism, sexism, and offensively provocative humor. Again, *cater your jokes to your audience.* Some obvious DON'Ts include: **don't** mock religion if you're performing at a church; **don't** joke about your divorce if you're performing at someone's wedding; and **don't** make crude sex jokes. Comedy shows are popular date spots — no need to ruin a couple's evening before they make it back home.

6. DON'T STEAL JOKES.

Only use your own material. Enough said.

Check out the following **websites and articles** for more tips on improving your own writing:

- 5 Secrets for Improving Your Comedy Writing by Fred Rubin:
  http://scriptfrenzy.org/node/413100
- This Stopped Being Funny Three Minutes Ago: Things I've Learned Writing Sketch
  Comedy by Jon Wolanske: http://scriptfrenzy.org/node/3160207
- YouTube tutorial about starting out in entertainment by Joe Pauly:
  http://www.youtube.com/watch?v=2RRj6ZwqX28&feature=related
- Writing Sketches by Richard Herring, David Mitchell and Robert Webb:
  http://www.guardian.co.uk/books/2008/sep/22/comedy2
- Comedy Writing and Timing by Brad Montgomery:
  http://www.bradmontgomery.com/general/comedy-writing-and-timing/
- Improve Yourself by Mike Bent: http://www.netplaces.com/comedy-writing/the-scouts-
  were-right-be-prepared/improve-yourself.htm

Chapter 6: How To Hustle

Networking & Job Hunting Tips For Comedians

I generate most of my own publicity. I don't have an agent or manager. The best way to network is to have relationships with fellow comedians. There are comedians who will say "Hey I think you're really funny, I'd like to book you." Just be funny. Get good. Everyone will come to you and want to be associated with you. It doesn't matter if you're a man, a woman, gay, straight, black, white, Asian, Latino. It's a meritocracy. If you're funny, you'll go really far. If you aren't funny… you won't. There's nothing wrong with networking; but if you present yourself to an agent or manager out of the blue they won't want to listen. If you're funny, everyone will come to you."

To give you a little background about the world of comedy: comedians in general are a bunch of sociopathic, alcoholic, drug addicted, prescription-drug-addled, petulant, narcissistic misanthropes. Keep in mind, this applies to many people in show business, not just comedians.

Shortly after I moved to New York, I was invited to join a Comics Round Table of ten comedians. It was the most awful experience imaginable. Nobody laughed at any of each other's jokes. Of course, I laughed at all the jokes, because I love to laugh. But comedians are notorious for not laughing when they're off stage. I was seen as the weak link in the Round Table, even though my stuff was already killing in clubs. They even held a "remedial" meeting for two comedians whom they thought were the weakest, and I was one of them. Needless to say, the group self-destructed. Fast forward several years, and the proof is in the pudding – eight of them are not doing comedy anymore, and I am much more successful than the ninth.

A big part of the comedian mentality is "I made it on my own without help, and I'm not helping you." There's a lot of that in the comedy business. It's dog eat dog. I know this firsthand. When I started out, I was part of an online forum that was absolutely awful. I was the target of a tremendous amount of vitriol because of the ethnic nature of my act. Now that I have a successful career, the last thing I want to do is waste my time trading insults with a bunch of comedians who are bitter, jaded and angry because their careers have gone nowhere.

You want to become a doctor? Lawyer? Accountant? You know what tests you have to take and how long you have to be in school. But there's no one right or wrong way to be a *comedian. There's also a preparation and study period where you have to pay your dues before you can find jobs. Perform as much as you can in as many venues as you can. I used to drive 50 miles to Orange County to perform at Alcoholics Anonymous meetings. I've performed at senior citizens homes. I've performed at cancer wards around New York. I've done Toastmasters meetings and parties.*

The main thing is to get up as much as you can and perform everywhere you can. Even if you aren't making money. Bringer shows are also a great way to get out there. They'll put up anybody if they can bring a crowd; they need to make money, sell tickets, fill the seats. Sometimes people will put themselves on stage and they just aren't funny at all, but at bringer shows they'll put professional comedians at the end so the audience will laugh. An open mic is great because anybody can get on, and it's a great way to get stage time in the beginning. Just keep getting up on stage over and over and over again.

Thousands of comics are begging to get on stage every day, yet the typical comedian in New York makes about $25 for a weekday performance, and $75 on a weekend. Which means that to make money in this business, you've got to get on stage a *lot*. It's crucial to your success as a stand-up comedian that you meet as many people as possible.

More information on social networking sites will be provided in **Chapter 17**, but here are a couple networking tips to get you started:

1. Make a list of people you know in the entertainment industry.

Set up lunches, phone calls, or coffee dates with as many people as you can. Sit down with them and pick their brains. If it feels appropriate, offer to send your resume along and see if they can pass it on.

2. Use LinkedIn.

It's a website *dedicated* to networking. Your colleagues can introduce you to other comedians or you can display your resume, YouTube clips, Twitter, and/or websites that feature you. You can also join groups related to entertainment and stay up to date on comedy-related news.

3. Tweet.

Twitter is a wonderfully open place to communicate with people. If you see a great show or like what a particular comedian is doing, tweet at them and let them know. They just might remember you — or at least bother to check out your page. And tweet back at people who mention you. Their fans may begin to recognize your name.

4. Bring friends.

The more guests you bring to shows where you are performing, the more the club owners will want you to come back. Why? Because comedy clubs have a two drink minimum. That's how they make money. *Every person you bring will purchase two drinks.* The more you bring business to a comedy club, the more the club owners and booking managers will notice you.

5. Offer yourself up as an opening act or an MC.

Have a friend who's throwing a party? Know a band that's performing? Offer to be their opening act at no charge. Getting exposure for yourself in any way you can is productive and furthers your chances of getting noticed elsewhere. You never know when a stranger will drop your name.

6. Use The Resources Available to You

As a comedian, it's imperative to know the basics of the Internet – for job hunting and networking alike. Something as small as accumulating YouTube views can help you get gigs. Additionally, there are many resources online for finding opportunities for performance and recognition.

The following websites are great places to find **open mic nights** and **comedy opportunities** in your area:

- http://www.chucklemonkey.com is a comprehensive database for open mic nights, although the listings can be out of date sometimes. Make sure to call the booking agent or comedy club before going to an open mic night listed on Chucklemonkey.
- http://www.comedyopenmics.com which sometimes redirects tohttp://www.comedyhunt.com is another fairly comprehensive guide to open mic opportunities.
- http://www.comedy.openmikes.org is a searchable site that provides a comprehensive list of upcoming open mic nights by location.
- http://www.thecomicscomic.com has a great listing of shows in and around New York City.
- http://www.dead-frog.com/live_comedy is a great way to search for comedy shows by zip code and find comedy in your area.

- http://badslava.com/comedy-mics.htm has listings for open mics in the major cities of 38 states.
- http://www.entertainmentcareers.net is a more comprehensive database that lists careers in the entertainment industry. Getting a job in entertainment (while you wait for the cash flow from your comedy career to start pouring in) is a great way to build connections.

7. Stay away from destructive environments

While networking online is a net positive, some online communities can be more destructive than helpful. Forums, especially anonymous ones, can turn into places where failing or struggling comedians gather to complain about why they aren't making it in the comedy world.

Comedians are odd people, and forums like http://alt.comedy.com and http://rec.forum can turn into corrosive environments. Here's a good rule of thumb to remember: successful comedians spend their time writing, working on their websites, traveling extensively and trying to book new work. They have no time to bicker back and forth in online forums. The most successful comedians don't *waste time* online. They use that time to write jokes. You should too.

Chapter 7: Getting Gigs

Performing Domestically

While New York and Los Angeles are famous for their comedy scene, there are comedy clubs everywhere. To tour full time as a stand-up comedian is to perform at all of these clubs — small and large. Whenever you are traveling in a new city, check out the nearest comedy club and practice an open mic night in front of strangers. Or visit premiere spots in each city and watch the pros perform.

To save you some Googling time, here's an alphabetical list of some of the country's best known comedy clubs:

Comedy clubs in (most) major cities:

- Albuquerque, The Box Performance Space & Improv Theatre
  - http://www.theboxabq.com/
- Appleton, WI – Skyline Comedy Cafe
  - http://www.rooftopcomedy.com/clubs/skyline
- Arlington, VA – All Stars Comedy Club
  - http://allstarscomedy.com/
- Aspen, CO – Wheeler Opera House
  - http://www.rooftopcomedy.com/clubs/wheeler
- Atlanta, GA – The Punchline, Laughing Skull Lounge
  - http://www.punchline.com/
  - http://www.rooftopcomedy.com/clubs/LaughingSkull
  - http://www.vortexcomedy.com/
- Atlantic City – The Borgata
  - http://www.theborgata.com/
- Austin, TX – The Velveeta Room
  - http://www.rooftopcomedy.com/clubs/velveetaroom
- Baltimore, MD – Drop Three, Sully's Comedy Cellar, Baltimore Comedy Factory

- http://dropthree.com/
- http://www.sullyscomedycellar.com/
- http://www.baltimorecomedy.com/

- Baton Rouge, LA – The Funny Bone Comedy Club, Phil Brady's Bar and Grill

- http://www.funnybonebatonrouge.com/
- http://www.philbradys.org/

- Birmingham, AL – Stardome

- http://www.rooftopcomedy.com/clubs/stardome

- Boise, ID – Hijinx Comedy Club, Funny Bone Comedy Club

- http://www.myspace.com/hijinxcomedyclub
- http://www.yelp.com/biz/funny-bone-comedy-club-boise

- Boston, MA – Motley's

- www.mottleyscomedy.com

- Boise, ID – Hijinx Comedy Club, Funny Bone Comedy Club

- http://www.myspace.com/hijinxcomedyclub
- http://www.yelp.com/biz/funny-bone-comedy-club-boise

- Boston, MA – Motley's
- Buffaly, NY – Doin' Time Comedy, Rob's Comedy Playhouse

- http://buffalocomedy.com/
- http://www.robscomedyplayhouse.com/

- Chapel Hill – DSI Comedy Theater, Goodnight's Comedy Club

- http://www.dsicomedytheater.com/
- http://www.goodnightscomedy.com/

- Charlotte, NC – The Comedy Zone

- http://www.cltcomedyzone.com

- Chicago, IL – Chicago Underground, The Lincoln Lodge, Second City

- http://www.theundergroundchicago.com/
- http://www.rooftopcomedy.com/clubs/lincolnlodge
- http://www.secondcity.com

- Cincinnati, OH – Go Bananas

  o http://www.rooftopcomedy.com/clubs/gobananas

- Cleveland, OH – Hilarities 4th Street Theatre

  o http://pickwickandfrolic.com/

- Columbus, OH – Columbus Funny Bone, Shadowbox

  o http://funnybonecentral.com/
  o http://www.shadowboxlive.org/

- Dallas/Forth Worth, TX – Back door, Hyena's, Ad-libs

  o http://www.backdoorcomedy.com/index
  o http://hyenascomedynightclub.com/dallas.html
  o http://www.ad-libs.com/

- D.C. – D.C. Improv, All Stars Comedy Club, Laugh Out Loud @ Club Elite, Gross National Product Comedy Group

  o http://www.improv.com
  o http://allstarscomedy.com/
  o http://www.laughoutloudmd.com/
  o http://gnpcomedy.com/

- Denver, CO – Comedy Works Denver, Denver Improv, Bovine Metropolis Theater

  o http://www.comedyworks.com
  o http://www.improvdenver.com
  o http://www.bovinemetropolis.com

- Detroit, MI – Coco's House of Comedy, Mark Ridley's Comedy Castle

  o http://www.yelp.com/biz/cocos-house-of-comedy-detroit
  o http://www.comedycastle.com/

- Hartford, CT – Brew Ha Ha Comedy Club, Steve Wronker's Funny Business, Hartford Funny Bone

  o http://www.citysteambrewerycafe.com/
  o http://www.swfb.net/
  o http://hartfordfunnybone.com/

- Houston, TX – The Comedy Showcase, Comedy Sportz Houston, Third Coast Comedy

  - http://www.thecomedyshowcase.com
  - http://www.comedysportzhouston.com
  - http://www.thirdcoastcomedy.com

- Indianapolis, IN – Crackers

  - http://www.rooftopcomedy.com/clubs/crackers

- Jacksonville, FL – Bonkers Comedy, The Comedy Zone
- Kansas City, KS – Stanford's

  - http://www.stanfordscomedyclub.com/

- Las Vegas, NV – Bonkerz, The Las Vegas Comedy Show

  - http://www.palacestation.com
  - http://www.thelasvegascomedyshow.com

- Long Island, NY – Governor's is comedy

  - http://www.govs.govs.com

- Los Angeles, CA – The Laugh Factory, The Comedy Store, Nerdist, Groundlings, Upright Citizens Brigade, Hollywood Improv, The Ice House

  - http://www.laughfactory.com/
  - http://thecomedystore.com/
  - http://www.meltcomics.com/blog/
  - http://www.groundlings.com/
  - http://losangeles.ucbtheatre.com/
  - http://www.improv.com/ComedyClub/Hollywood
  - http://icehousecomedy.com/index.cfm

- Louisville, Kentucky – Improv

  - http://www.improv.com

- Miami, FL – Improv, Just the Funny

  - www.improv.com
  - http://www.justthefunny.com

- Minneapolis, MN – Acme Comedy Company

- http://twincities.metromix.com/leisure/comedy/acme-comedy-company-north-loop/337053/content

- Milwaukee – Jokerz Comedy Club, Milwaukee Comedy Cafe, Comedy Sportz Milwaukee

  - http://www.jokerzcomedyclub.com/
  - http://milwaukeescomedycafe.com/
  - http://www.comedysportzmilwaukee.com/main_page.html

- Nashville, TN – Zanies, Bar Car, Nashville Comedy Theater

  - http://www.nashville.zanies.com
  - http://www.nashvillecomedytheater.com/

- New Jersey, NJ – Vinnie Brand's Stress Factory, The Comedy Cabaret, Uncle Vinnie's Comedy Club, Bananas Comedy Club

  - http://www.stressfactory.com
  - http://comedycabaret.com/
  - http://www.unclevinniescomedyclub.com/
  - http://bananascomedyclub.com/

- New Orleans, LA – The National Comedy Company, La Nuit Comedy Theater, Le Chat Noir

  - http://www.nationalcomedycompany.com/The_National_Comedy_Company/NCC_Comedy
  - http://lanuittheater.com/
  - http://www.cabaretlechatnoir.com/

- New York, NY – Gotham, Caroline's, Comic Strip Live

  - http://gothamcomedyclub.com/
  - http://www.carolines.com/
  - http://www.rooftopcomedy.com/clubs/comicstriplive

- Oklahoma City, OK – OKC Comedy Club, Loony Bin

  - http://okccomedy.com/
  - http://www.loonybincomedy.com/

- Orange County, CA – Clean Corporate Comedy, Secret City Comics Society, The Dinner Detective Murder Mystery Comedy Show

  - http://cleancorporatecomedy.com

- http://www.secretcitycomedy.com/
- thedinnerdetective.com

- Orlando, FL – SAK Comedy Lab, The Improv Orlando, Bonkerz Comedy Club

- http://www.sak.com
- http://theimprovorlando.com/
- http://bonkerzcomedy.com/

- Phoenix, AZ – The Comedy Spot, The Torch Theatre, Standup Live, Clean Comedy Club

- http://www.thecomedyspot.net/
- http://www.thetorchtheatre.com/
- http://standuplive.com/index.cfm
- http://www.cleancomedyclub.com/

- Pittsburgh, PA – Funny Bone

- http://funnybonepgh.com/

- Philadelphia, PA – The Comedy Cabaret, The Laff House, Helium Comedy Club, Chuckles Comedy

- http://comedycabaret.com/
- http://laffhouse.com/
- http://heliumcomedy.com/
- http://www.chucklescomedy.com/

- Portland, OR – Curious Comedy, The Unscriptables, Helium Comedy Club

- http://www.curiouscomedy.org/
- http://www.theunscriptables.com/
- http://heliumcomedy.com/

- Richmond, VA – Funny Bone, 9:55, Rita's Comedy Club

- http://www.richmondfunnybone.com/
- http://www.955comedy.com/
- http://www.ritascomedyclub.com/

- Sacramento, CA – Laughs Unlimited, Punchline

- http://www.laughsunlimited.com/
- http://www.punchlinecomedyclub.com/

- Salt Lake City, UT – Wiseguys Comedy

  o http://wiseguyscomedy.com

- San Antonio, TX – River Center Comedy Club, Laugh Out Loud Comedy Club, Oxymorons Improv Troupe

  o http://www.rivercentercomedyclub.com/
  o http://www.lolsanantonio.com/
  o http://www.oxymoronsimprov.com/

- San Diego, CA – The Comedy Palace, Mad House Comedy Club, National Comedy Theater

  o http://www.thecomedypalace.com/
  o http://madhousecomedyclub.com/
  o http://www.nationalcomedy.com/

- San Francisco, CA – The Punch Line, SF Standup, Cobb's Comedy Club, Rooftop at Large

  o http://www.punchlinecomedyclub.com/
  o http://www.sfstandup.com/
  o http://www.cobbscomedyclub.com/
  o http://www.rooftopcomedy.com/clubs/rooftopatlarge

- Savannah, GA – CHT Entertainment, Hard Hearted Hannah's Playhouse, The Gypsy Comedy Club

  o http://chtentertainment.com/
  o http://www.hardheartedhannahsplayhouse.com/
  o http://thegypsycomedyclub.com/new_page_20.htm

- Seattle, WA – Comedy Underground, Laughs Comedy Club

  o http://comedyunderground.com/seattle/open_mic.php
  o http://www.laughscomedy.com/

- St. Louis – Laughs on The Landing, House of Comedy Saint Louis, The Billiken Club, Funny Bone Comedy Club

  o laughsonthelanding.com
  o http://www.houseofcomedy.net/
  o http://thebillikenclub.wordpress.com/
  o http://stlouisfunnybone.com/

- Tampa, FL - Side Splitters

   ○ http://www.rooftopcomedy.com/clubs/sidesplitters

Or check out the following three websites to access databases of comedy clubs around the US:

- http://www.rooftopcomedy.com/clubs is a great website for finding comedy clubs in your area.
- http://www.stand-upcomedians.com/comedy-info/comedy-clubs/ allows you to download a free PDF of comedy clubs in your area.
- http://en.wikipedia.org/wiki/Comedy_club has a large list of prominent comedy clubs around the world.

Opportunities To Perform For Up-And-Coming Stand-Up Comedians

Gotham Comedy Club in New York is pretty much the number one comedy club around. My other favorites are Hilarities Comedy Club in Cleveland, Ohio and Parlor Live in Bellevue, just outside of Seattle, Washington. They treat the comedians well. They're packed with a great crowd of 300-400 people. These clubs are both part of a bigger entertainment extravaganza. You've got a comedy show, billiards, karaoke, and a restaurant. There's a real festive environment and it's a lot of fun. Outside of New York or LA, most comedy clubs are the same: 200-300 seats and usually part of the Improv chain.

Comedy Festivals

In Trinidad and Tobago I once performed in a stadium at a Carnivale comedy festival. I also perform at the Calgary Comedy Festival every year. Comedy festivals are fantastic. They can be a scam, with organizers putting all their friends in the lineup and then sending out mass emails all over the world saying "Come to the Boston Comedy Festival and perform! Send us $35 and we'll look at your tape." They have thousands of comedians pay $35 to audition. Then you have to fly yourself there, put yourself up, pay for your own meals, and perform for nothing.

However, they can be a great way to meet and network with other comedians in the very beginning. And there are some legitimate prizes. A lot of them pay $25,000 to the most popular comedian. I would highly recommend comedy festivals for people starting out. While flying yourself to one may not be a good investment, it's probably a good idea to check out local festivals — even if you don't win.

Comedy festivals are a great way to get lots of exposure, meet fellow comedians, and get your foot in the proverbial comedy door. If you are traveling abroad, these festivals can be a great opportunity to immerse yourself and learn from fellow comedians. Below is a list of prominent **comedy festivals** from both the domestic and international scenes.

- Washington DC Comedy Festival
- Portland Comedy Festival
- Edinburgh Comedy Festival
- Montreal Just For Laughs Comedy Festival
- Melbourne International Comedy Festival
- Calgary Comedy Festival
- Boston Comedy Festival

Performing Internationally

The UK is the next best place outside of the US to do comedy. The UK has The Comedy Store (unaffiliated with The Comedy Store in Los Angeles), which is absolutely fantastic. UK clubs pay much more than clubs in the US.

Comedy is still an American art form that hasn't really spread outside of the English speaking atmosphere, although The Comedy Store just opened a branch in Bombay, India. Take Out Comedy also recently opened in Hong Kong. As evidenced by the pun on Chinese food, most comedy clubs outside the US cater to English speaking clientele.

By and large my comedy shows are for an English-speaking audience. That said, many of my clients are South or East Asian, which is a good audience for me because I understand that humor. I speak French, Dutch, Japanese, and Spanish. But I don't think I could pull off a comedy act in another language. That doesn't exclude me from the International comedy market. I've been hired to do everything from corporate events in Dubai at the Emirates Golf Club to someone's 25th anniversary party in Hong Kong to a tourist resort in Mexico.

Performing internationally is a whole different ball game. Different cultures are receptive to different types of humor, and you should definitely do your research on which clubs are receptive to your style. To get you started, here are some prominent **International Comedy Clubs**:

- Hong Kong – Take Out Comedy
  - http://www.takeoutcomedy.com/site/
- London – Jongleurs, The Comedy Store
  - http://www.jongleurs.com/
  - http://www.thecomedystore.co.uk/
- Dublin – Anseo Comedy Club
  - http://laughoutloud.ie/
- Manchester – XS Comedy Club
  - http://www.xsmalarkey.com/

- Edinburgh – The Stand

  - http://www.rooftopcomedy.com/clubs/thestand

- Toronto – Second City

  - www.secondcity.com

- Amsterdam – Boom Chicago, Comedy Cafe

  - http://www.iamsterdam.com/en/locations/boom-chicago/1eee951f-fb70-88a7-c24a2dad74c576bf?

  - http://www.iamsterdam.com/en/placestogo/comedy-caf/9a7b87f2-009e-4fea-b313-8d0d49d548cb

Colleges And Universities

Colleges are fantastic places for comedy. You have student activity representatives on every college campus — big or small. They will pay a lot of money. Rutgers paid $15,000 to have Snooki come and speak – that's just how celebrity works. Every year there are conventions where you can meet 2,000 college representatives at once. A comedian can perform at these and suddenly be mobbed with tons of colleges and book $100,000 worth of shows. Bill Clinton makes $250,000 per speech. It just goes to show: when you get well known you can make a huge living simply by speaking.

Here are some great colleges and universities for comedy:

- Auburn University
- Barnard College
- Brown University
- California State University Los Angeles
- Columbia University
- City University of New York
- Cuyahoga Community College
- Drexel University
- Florida Tech
- Georgetown University
- George Washington University
- Hope College
- Indiana University
- Kean University
- Keio University Tokyo
- Lehigh University
- Loyola University
- Montclair State University
- Mount Sinai School of Medicine
- New York University
- Northwestern University
- Ohio State University
- Oklahoma State University

- Penn State University
- Seton Hall University
- Southern Methodist University
- Stanford University
- Stevens Institute of Technology
- SUNY Binghamton
- SUNY Stony Brook
- University of Connecticut
- University of Alabama
- University of Florida
- University of Chicago
- University of Georgia
- University of Maryland
- University of Michigan
- University of New Hampshire
- University of Salford, Manchester, England
- University of Virginia
- Washington University
- Williams College
- Portland State University
- University of Texas at Dallas

Chapter 9: Performing Live

How To Kill It On Stage

On a whim, I went to the grand opening of the new branch of the Laugh Factory in New York a couple years ago with someone from my comedy class. When we got there I spoke to the doorman. I told him I was clean and that I'd recently worked with Robert Schimmel — just a little bit about myself. Then I asked if I could go take a look inside.

We went upstairs and Artie Lang was upstairs talking about going to the bathroom in his pants and leaving his pants on the side of the road. Nobody was laughing. I looked at the audience and they were all older folks in tuxedos. They just weren't digging it. Bob Saget was the headliner, from America's Funniest Home Videos. He has one of the filthiest, dirtiest potty mouths in comedy. After Saget got up the owner saw me in the hallway and said "You are clean, right?" remembering that I'd mentioned it to the doorman.

He sent me up for five minutes, gave Bob a note asking him to announce me as the next comedian. I tore the roof off the place. They let me go on as long as I wanted. I was doing well because my stuff works better for older people and people who don't like dirty humor. Bob Saget is much funnier than I am, but my stuff just worked better that night. Afterwards Bob Saget said to the owner "Hey, this guy's hilarious. I want him to open for me all weekend!" So I opened for Bob all weekend, which was a great opportunity.

Recognize that you will always be nervous. Nervousness is natural and there's nothing you can do about that. Don't feel bad about being nervous. Do not get messed up beforehand. Don't do drugs and don't get drunk because they will never help you perform. You don't need to. Simply tough it out. It will be more rewarding in the end. One of my favorite sayings is: there's no feeling you can't get on drugs that you can't get without drugs.

No matter how much you have rehearsed, performing live is nerve-wracking. Many people get nervous and anxious, and stand-up comedy is a hard career path to choose if you are one of these people. But being nervous is natural. Accept your nervousness. Recognize it and sit with it for a moment. You can't know how the crowd will react, but you *can* prepare yourself to face them.

Dan's Best Tips For Live Performing:

1. Know your material.

Rehearse, rehearse, rehearse. Have more material than you give the audience. Have backup jokes and possible tangents to go on in case the audience finds one topic particularly funny.

2. Bring some friends.

It's always good to have a couple unconditional supporters. And the club owner and bartender will thank you afterwards for the business.

3. Arrive early. And sober.

Learn the room. Walk around and practice speaking if you have the chance. Listen to the acoustics, orient yourself on stage, and make yourself at home before your performance.

4. Relax.

Picture the audience in their underwear. Or just stop worrying about them and introduce yourself to calm your nerves.

5. Realize that people want to have fun.

They came to laugh. Unless it's an open mic night filled with bitter, unsuccessful comedians who came to practice their own material and not listen, then the audience came intending to have fun. So get to know them, open up a dialogue with the audience and ask if they're enjoying themselves. The way you talk to the audience, especially as a beginner, is often more important than how successful your jokes are. If they like you, they'll laugh.

6. Don't apologize.

Have confidence, even if you have to fake it. The audience probably didn't notice whatever it was that you *think* you did wrong.

7. Don't worry if you bomb.

The inexperienced comedian will inevitably start to fall apart. He or she will speed up, get nervous, or start moving through jokes without correctly delivering punch lines. The key to overcoming this is to **always have a back pocket joke**. The emergency joke that you know will work. If you need to, write it down and literally keep it in your back pocket.

Chapter 8: Rehearsing Your Routine . . .

And How To Make It Look Like You Didn't

My teachers always say that when you're doing comedy right, you're giving the audience the impression that you're making it up off the top of your head. Plenty of audience members actually think that. But it's an illusion.

These are jokes that you've done over and over, hundreds of times. I do a lot of the same jokes for senior citizens that I do for young boys because what's the likelihood that the same two people will be at those shows? Slim to none. In the beginning, the challenge is to string together five minutes of jokes. Sit there, type it out, and then say your first joke, which leads to your second joke, then your third joke, and so on. Hopefully it's organized in a coherent fashion. Arrange the jokes in a cohesive way.

Anybody can memorize five minutes of stuff. You're never going to do five minutes and have someone come up and say "Hey, can you headline my club for an hour?" I learned how to rollerblade backwards down stairs and now I can rollerblade down 100 stairs without thinking about it, but in the beginning I went off a curb and did one at a time. Then I did two stairs and I fell all the time. But I built it up little by little very slowly. Similarly, when you start doing comedy you do 5 minutes. The next time you do 7-10. Then you get to 15. Getting to 20 is a really big milestone because you can then feature at a comedy club for a headliner.

As you get closer to becoming an experienced, full-time stand-up comedian, rehearsal will occur more on stage than off stage. There'll be less pacing your living room trying to memorize your jokes line by line, and more actually making jokes you've practiced before.

The first time you get on stage you won't do more than 5-7 minutes. Then you will graduate to 10 minutes, most likely including a significant portion of your original 5-7 minutes in your 10 minute act. You will graduate from 10 minutes to 12, 12 to 15, and then 15 to 20. You'll add on little by little as you build your act while perfecting the material you've already performed.

To repeat: the best rehearsal happens on stage. You get practice both delivering jokes and reacting to the audience. That said, you can't rely on getting stage time, whether it be at open mic events or at booked gigs, in order to rehearse your material. You've got to practice on your own. The following tips will help you get started:

1. Develop a routine.

Wake up early and practice for a half-hour. Or simply get into the habit of telling yourself jokes as you make breakfast, shower, or perform any other daily activity. This practice is habit forming and will help you get comfortable with your jokes.

2. Make a timeline.

When are your next performances? How much material do you need to memorize? Ideally, you will have everything memorized the night before your show. How many minutes do you need to memorize per day in order to accomplish these goals?

3. Practice with a microphone.

Get used to holding and using the mic before you stand in front of an audience. If you haven't practiced with a microphone before, it can feel heavy and awkward. It will negatively affect your body language and the way in which you come across to the audience. Additionally, it is important to practice holding the mic an appropriate distance from your mouth: too far away and no one will hear you, too close and your words will sound muffled and cacophonous. This varies from mic to mic; nevertheless, practicing on *any* mic will significantly improve your performance.

4. Tape yourself.

See what you look like and mark sections that you need to improve on. Did you make a weird face one minute and 33 seconds into your act when you made that joke about your ex-boyfriend or girlfriend? Although it can be excruciating, taping yourself and reviewing your performance can help you get the little kinks out of your act and help you perform confidently on stage.

Chapter 10: Stand Up Anywhere

Different Avenues For Performance

Thousands of comedians are willing to perform for nothing in New York or LA. Outside of those two cities, though, the clubs are smaller and less prestigious. A comedian who is resourceful and who can organize his or her own shows by thinking of out-of-the-box places to perform can find an infinite number of opportunities.

I'm booked by an agency that hires voices to be actors on the radio. I only do about 30-50 phone calls a year, but sometimes I'll do voices. The best one that I'm known for is Bill Clinton. I wrote a bit about Bill Clinton being in the hospital once and got told it was too intelligent and I had to make it all about sex. I did 30 calls in my underwear from 5am-10am pretending to be Bill Clinton in the hospital. People thought it was really him.

If you listen to the radio, these morning shows have bits where someone's cheating on his wife and then they catch him red-handed, etc. I've done a lot of calls like that. The guy who pretends to send flowers for the wife. One of my most famous calls is the Indian guy cheating on his wife with a white woman. There's one about an Arab selling peanuts on the street in New York: "People are getting sick on your nuts! They found a hair on your nuts!"

I've also done a tremendous number of radio interviews. When I was touring with the late Robert Schimmel he'd bring me with him to go on the radio. There's a lot of opportunity on the radio.

We've already touched on open mic nights and comedy clubs, which are the most typical venues for stand-up. But there's no reason you should always have to compete with thousands of other comedians to get both practice and experience. Being inventive about places to perform, and taking initiative when it comes to getting exposure, is a key to your success. Television, radio, and special events are all great venues outside of comedy clubs where you can get some exposure and work your magic.

Television comedy writing has its roots in stand-up. Many full-time comedy writers were once stand-up comedians, or started at groups such as The Upright Citizens Bridge or The Groundlings. Watching comedy on TV, reading scripts, taking TV writing classes, passing around writing samples of your work, and following TV writers on Twitter are great ways to reach out to former and current performers to find new venues for performance.

Comedians often make weekly podcasts that they release via iTunes or make available on their own websites. Podcasts are a great way to put yourself out there without having to worry about what you look like or if you ever got over that nervous twitch you were working on last week.

They're also great avenues to explore comedic conversation. Recruit other aspiring comedian friends and make your own podcasts for distribution, or do research to see if any of your favorite podcasts are giving listeners a chance to get on the air.

To get you started, here are some of the co-authors' favorite comedy podcasts as well as some additional information below:

- Adam Corolla
- http://www.adamcarolla.com/
- Never not funny
- http://pardcast.com/
- WTF with Marc Maron
- http://www.wtfpod.com/
- The Ricky Gervais Podcast
- http://www.rickygervais.com/podcast.php
- Comedy and Everything Else
- http://www.jimmydorecomedy.com/show/comedy-and-everything-else
- The Greg Fitzsimmons experience
- http://www.gregfitzsimmons.com/
- Louis C.K.'s podcasts
- http://itunes.apple.com/us/podcast/louis-c.k.-comedian/id208961993
- Comedy Bang! Bang!
- http://www.earwolf.com/show/comedy-bang-bang-podcast/
- The Nerdist
- http://www.nerdist.com/category/podcast/
- Pod F. Tompkast

- ○ http://pft.libsyn.com/

- How Was Your Week?

- ○ http://howwasyourweek.libsyn.com/

- Uhh Yeah Dude

- ○ http://uhhyeahdude.com/

New comedy podcasts get released everyday. But here are a few interesting articles covering *today's* popular podcasts:

- Rolling Stone Magazine's 10 Best Comedy Podcasts of The Moment:
- ○ http://www.rollingstone.com/culture/news/the-10-best-comedy-podcasts-of-the-moment-20110406

- Splitsider: A Seriously Comprehensive Guide to Comedy Podcasts
- ○ http://splitsider.com/2011/01/a-seriously-comprehensive-guide-to-comedy-podcasts

- A full list of podcasts by comedians on the Home Box Office TV Network:
- ○ http://www.hbo.com/podcasts/standup/podcast.xml

- A USA Today Editorial on the Top 10 Comedy Podcasts:
- ○ http://content.usatoday.com/communities/popcandy/post/2011/02/a-pop-podcast-primer-my-top-10-comedy-podcasts/1

Outside of podcasts, there are tons of other inventive, offthebeaten track ways to get yourself out there. Senior citizens' homes, Alcoholics Anonymous and Narcotics Anonymous meetings, corporate conventions, country clubs, temples, churches, hospitals, and schools are all great places to practice your act and gain exposure.

And of course comedy clubs aren't the only nightlife spots looking for funny people to get up on stage. Bars, burlesque or neo-burlesque clubs, and performance theaters often have stand-up acts. Also keep an eye out for charity events, conferences, Bar and Bat Mitzvahs, birthday parties, and weddings where you might be able to perform.

Even if you aren't performing as a headlining comedian, offering to be an event MC is also great experience. You'll be able to practice a few of your jokes without the pressure of creating a whole act of your own.

While you may not get paid for all these oddball gigs, the exposure is priceless. More importantly, each act will help you progress toward your ultimate goal of becoming a full-time stand-up comedian. Just make sure to think outside the box and come up with your own list of places near you!

Chapter 11: A Day In The Life

Touring And Performing As A Full-Time Stand-Up Comedian

Once you achieve any modicum of success as a comedian, you'll begin to travel a lot. It's a huge barrier to a lot of people who despise travel and can't take it. If you don't like travel you shouldn't get into this job full time.

Being open to travel hugely increases your opportunities. I'm in at least 1-2 hotels every weekend. In the beginning it's a lot of driving: people will drive 100s of miles to make $150 on a gig. It's not a profitable enterprise by any means.

Lots of comedy clubs are low budget. They treat their comedians like dirt, put us up in seedy motels or condos with other comedians who are doing drugs or drinking or bringing girls back to get action. But if you clean up your act and perform at corporate events you can get put up in a hotel, make 100 times what you make at a club, and eat filet mignon while you're at it. It's a total dichotomy. Guys who've been on Letterman and Leno all the time struggle to make 10-15 grand a year, while if you do corporate stuff you can get that in a night and not be a big name. It's incredible. But they're two different worlds, and the corporate world is a completely different animal.

The life of a touring stand-up comedian isn't routine and you have to be very flexible and accommodating in order to make it. Whether it be a domestic or an international comedy tour, you'll have two modes: performance mode and non-performance mode. You have to get used to both.

Traveling will often factor into your schedule in unpredictable ways. You should get up early enough to make it to the airport and through security, then use your wait time to review your upcoming schedule and make sure you know where you're going once you land.

Spend the time on your flight or train ride updating your web page or working on jokes. Chat with everyone you can, especially the person next to you. It's a great way to make friends and publicize yourself. Who knows? You might be sitting next to movers and shakers from all walks of life. Take public transportation or pick up a rental car, check into wherever you are staying, and take a nap or do something to clear your head before heading to the venue.

Arrive early. You'll need the time. Once you get to the venue, meet the client and make sure you've been paid. Insist on full payment: 50 percent when the show is booked and the other 50 percent upon arrival. Interface with the production and audiovisual staff and make sure everyone is on the same page. Test the mic and the lights to know your environment. Take a minute and re-read or rehearse your jokes to yourself once more. Then, once the crowd has arrived and settled, do what you do best: perform!

After the performance, the most important priority is to set up a table in the most strategic position possible. Try to make it so that everyone in the audience will have to pass you. Then give them all your business cards. You can generate a surprising amount of revenue selling CDs and DVDs. They cost about 77 cents per set, and you can sell them for around $20. Do the math: that's a profit of $19.23 per sale.

Handing out your business card is even more critical. Members of the audience will never remember a comedian's name. But they'll throw the card into their wallets or purses and come across it another time — perhaps when they want to book you!

You will likely be up late, usually until well after the show is over.

It's crucial to use your time wisely, on or off the road. There simply isn't enough time to get everything done. And you can always do more. A comedian's work day is filled with self-promotion, handling emails, negotiating shows, writing contracts, making travel reservations, and attending auditions. Not to mention practicing. And writing more jokes.

Chapter 12: The Nitty Gritty Details

Lifestyle, Salary, Perks, And Disadvantages

Your typical full-time comedian is faced with a tremendous number of disadvantages. Chief amongst them: extremely low income with no health insurance. If you aren't a big name, it can be sheer misery. A lot of comedians are struggling and have to have other full-time jobs. So they can't really tour because they have to be around. Those who have left their jobs are struggling to eat and pay rent. They spend the night at the airport instead of hotels. This is how things are for the majority of comedians who aren't well known. For the first 5-10 years it's extremely hard to make a living.

You kind of have to put your ego and self respect aside because you will get rejected. People who book shows will reject you. People who own clubs will reject you. Agents and managers will reject you. It's like dating — tons of rejection. By the way, if you're a comedian who's just starting off, good luck dating — especially if you're gone half the time and make no money. When you're a comedian you audition for commercials, television, movies and you don't even know why you're being rejected. You have to deal with a tremendous amount of rejection. Every day people are leaving the comedy world because they can't make a living, they're tired of the humiliation and degradation.

If you're a woman it's ten times worse. Women are funny but there are gigantic barriers to women that men don't have. Number one is the sexual harassment. Male comedians often try to be funny and they end up offensive. They'll harass female comedians and try to get them into bed. Female comedians on the road sleeping in seedy motels have to deal with an added element of personal danger.

Your lifestyle as a full-time stand-up comedian will depend on how many performances you can book as well as whether you are touring in this country or abroad. You have the benefit of organizing your own life and are ultimately in charge of your own schedule.

Full-time stand-up comedians are like independent contractors: they book gigs whenever and wherever they can. While a comedian's schedule can resemble that of a band on tour, it differs from a band in that promoters aren't necessary in order to set up shows around the country. Some high profile comedians do have talent agents who help them get commercial and film auditions as well as managers who book performances for them. But social networking and the Internet have rendered these services unnecessary.

Before the Internet, comedians had to work with agents to get commercial and film auditions. They'd also have to work with agents to get on prominent comedy-related television programming like late night talk shows, Comedy Central shows, or premium cable channels like HBO.

In recent years, however, Internet-enabled disintermediation has fundamentally altered the comedy space. Disintermediation — or the elimination of middlemen — allows comedians to create their own publicity. Today, a comedian can put something on YouTube and get noticed right away. If people like your act, it spreads around the world. Comedy clubs, bookers, and promoters will reach out to *you*, getting rid of the need for an agent or manager. Bonus: if you don't have an agent, **you keep all your earnings for yourself**.

Agents and managers take up to 15% of a stand-up comedian's paycheck in exchange for their services, so choosing an agent is a big investment. If you do choose to get an agent, prominent agencies to consider are ones like William Morris Endeavor, Creative Artists Agency, United Talent Agency, and International Creative Management. Or you can go with booking agencies like Comedy Store Management and Summit Comedy, which focus more exclusively on comedians.

But let's be honest for a second: most aspiring comedians are starving. It's a competitive industry and it's very difficult to make a living as a comedian. The pay is lumpy and inconsistent.

That said, once you get to a certain level you'll get paid to be a tourist — making money to travel around the country (or the world) and perform at night. Sometimes this takes ten or twenty years. Sometimes less. Either way, be prepared to have a second income while you are first starting out.

Think of stand-up comedy as the roots of a tree that can blossom into many branches: there are a variety of careers you can get into with stand-up experience. Improv, print modeling, acting, writing, and event planning careers can all begin with stand-up. Think of it this way: people who start their own companies usually put in grueling 18 to 20 hour days when they are first starting out. Hard work is the linchpin of success, and if you think of your stand-up career as your own business, and put a similar amount of time and effort into it, your business will most likely flourish.

Chapter 13: Dressing The Part

www.hyperink.com

60

Dressing The Part

It's funny, I always ask my clients what I should wear, and they inevitably will say that since I'm the comedian, I can wear whatever I want. However, my teacher gave me a tip many years ago, which is to dress as well as the most well-dressed person in the audience. I think this is a great rule of thumb. Again, your typical comedian has no clue about how to dress. Comedians are notorious for dressing poorly both off and on stage. One thing I admired about Jerry Seinfeld is that he always wore a jacket and tie to every show. When I'm doing a corporate event, charity gala, wedding or whatever, I always, always wear a tie. The only time I will dress down in a T-shirt and jeans is if I'm doing a college event or B-level comedy club, where it's kind of expected.

This may seem trivial, but appearance is a fairly common issue in the world of stand-up comedy. In a nutshell: many comedians don't know how to dress.

Comedians are often cynical or self-deprecating. But they shouldn't look like this on stage. A good rule of thumb: you should always dress better than the best dressed person in your audience. This is fairly self explanatory. If you are performing at a wedding, wear a tuxedo. If you are performing at a corporate event, wear a suit. If you are performing at a comedy club, at least put on a button down. You may even try tucking in your shirt! It's very important to dress appropriately. Cater your clothing to your audience and you will immediately feel more comfortable on stage.

Should your material take precedence over your clothing? Of course. But that doesn't mean you shouldn't put thought into your appearance. You wouldn't wear a t-shirt to a corporate interview, so don't wear one to a comedy show. You're making an impression on the audience the moment you step out on stage, so it's probably not a good idea to wear sweatpants, sandals, or a t-shirt. Whatever you do, don't dress to be funny. You should be funny enough on your own, you don't need clothes to help you accomplish that.

Chapter 16: Comic Industry Inspirations

20 Great Comics

Inspiration is everywhere. But sometimes it helps to simply study the experts. The job requires a tremendous amount of focus and a lot of work, and getting caught up in the careers of others can be very detrimental. But it's important to look up to **comedians who inspire you**.

Here's a **Top 20 List** of some comedians — big and small, old and new — to follow (in no particular order):

1. Jerry Seinfeld. Movie/Television star and creator of the situational comedy, *Seinfeld*. Also a bona fide stand-up star. He's a comic, a classic, and a fantastic role-model.

2. Larry David. Speaking of *Seinfeld*... Larry David is also the star and creator of the show *Curb Your Enthusiasm*, which currently airs on HBO. No comic does as great a job as he does exposing the underlying tension and awkwardness of everyday situations.

3. Robert Schimmel. Famous for X-Rated and controversial material, Robert Schimmel was a regular guest on the Howard Stern show. While this isn't necessarily the type of comedy advocated in this book, respect must be paid to history's most successful stand-up comics — and Robert Schimmel was one of them.

3. Tina Fey. This SNL Veteran turned 30 Rock creator is an inspiration to female comics everywhere. She is hilarious, self-deprecating, and respectable. She's had some notorious trouble with Twitter, so you're better off just reading her recently published autobiography, *Bossypants*.

4. Bob Saget. America's Funniest Home Videos anyone? Who doesn't love seeing a toddler accidentally trip over a dog and splash into a baby pool that happens to be full of pee? Not to mention, Bob Saget's role as Mary-Kate & Ashely's father on *Full House* will keep him ingrained in our memories forever.

5. Bill Cosby. A classic stand-up comedian. After starting off in comedy clubs and proving himself on the stand-up stage, Cosby got his own sitcom: the situational comedy classic, *The Cosby Show*. If you haven't seen it, you should. Pay him a visit at http://www.billcosby.com/

6. Chris Rock. He may be profane, but rumor has it that in person he's the nicest guy you could imagine. He started working at the Catch a Rising Star comedy club chain in New York and worked his way up through the ranks, focusing mostly on class and race relations in the United States. He was voted 8th on Channel 4's 100 Great Stand-Ups in 2010. His HBO one-hour special *Kill The Messenger* is definitely worth watching. http://www.chrisrock.com/

7. Louis C.K. Irreverent, controversial, and brilliant, Louis C.K. is one of the most forward thinking comics around today. He relishes in awkwardness, self-deprecation, and no holds barred acts where he says what everyone else is afraid to say. He also brilliantly incorporates stand-up comedy in his new show *Louie*, currently airing on FX. Find him at http://www.louisck.net/. He sort of hates Twitter, but if you want to, you can follow him: @louisck.

8. Ricky Gervais. British. Hilarious. Creator of *The Office* (the British version). Host of the Golden Globes. http://www.rickygervais.com/. He tweets too: @rickygervais

9. Aziz Ansari. Better known as Tom Haverford on NBC's *Parks and Recreation*, this up-and-coming star has a great sense of humor. Check out his first one hour special from Comedy Central, *Intimate Moments for A Sensual Evening*, or follow him on Twitter (@azizansari) or Tumblr (http://azizisbored.tumblr.com/).

10. Ellie Kemper. Stanford grad, *The Office* actress, and UCB-trained stand-up comedian. Check her out on UCB here: http://www.ucbcomedy.com/talent/view/138/ellie-kemper

11. Jim Dailakis. Australian comedian who has headlined all over the world. At the very least you have to love him for his accent. Visit http://comedianjim.com/ to find out more.

12. Robin Williams. Flubber. Mrs. Doubtfire. The 2009 Weapons of Self-Destruction stand-up tour. Enough said. http://www.robinwilliams.com/

13. Amy Poehler. Another SNL Veteran, another sitcom star (playing Leslie Knope on NBC's *Parks and Recreation* alongside Aziz Ansari), and one of the founders of the Upright Citizens Brigade comedy troupe. Follow her @amypoehler or check out her amazing website.

14. Steve Martin. Steve Martin became famous for his stand-up in the 1970's on the Smothers Brothers Comedy Show before breaking into other forms of comedy and acting. He has since hosted the Academy Awards three times, starred in dozens of movies, and won Emmys, Grammys, and American Comedy Awards. What's not to admire? Follow him on Twitter @SteveMartinToGo or visit www.stevemartin.com for more details.

15. Eddie Murphy. Okay, so he dropped out of the Oscars for 2012. We're all bummed. But we'll forgive him because who doesn't love Eddie Murphy? Comedy Central does, as he was ranked #10 on their Top 100 Comedians of All Time list. Follow him: @80sEddieMurphy on Twitter.

16. Billy Crystal. It's only fair to mention Eddie Murphy's Oscar replacement next. Who doesn't love Billy Crystal? If you don't know, you should. Watch *When Harry Met Sally*, or this hilarious video from FunnyorDie.com to know more.

17. George Carlin. This guy has won five Grammy Awards for his comedy albums. He's revered by veterans and up-and-coming comedians alike. Enough said. http://www.georgecarlin.com/

18. Sarah Silverman. This bold and brash woman addresses subjects like racism, sexism, and religion in hilarious and daring ways. Originally an SNL writer and occasional performer, she branched out to create her own programming for Comedy Central: The Sarah Silverman Show. Go to www.sarahsilvermanonline.com or follow @SarahKSilverman on Twitter to know more.

19. Dave Chappelle. Sketch comedy king, impersonator extraordinaire, host of *Chappelle's Show*, which is still on the air despite its abrupt end in 2005. See for yourself : @_Dave_Chappelle.

20. Megan Amram. Last but not least: a young favorite. This up-and-coming, recent Harvard grad went from 5,000 to 25,000 followers in no time. And now she has about 119,000. Read her hilarious imagining of HBO's *Game of Thrones*here or just follow her on Twitter like the rest of us: @meganamram.

Chapter 17: Final Advice To Aspiring Comedians

Have Your Head In The Clouds But Your Feet On The Ground

If you want to do comedy or some other out of the box form of entertainment, it's really important to have your head in the clouds but your feet on the ground. You need to make a living and have a steady job or other form of income, or the struggle will get you down. Comedy or music are things you have to work years at before you make money.

According to Nielsen Ratings, the average American watches 34 hours of TV per week. On a Friday or Saturday night, they're probably going out because everyone else they know is going out. Then you go out, get drunk, get a hangover, and then the whole next day is shot before you rinse and repeat. Those are the hours you have to work on your craft, when everyone else is watching TV from the time they come home to the time they go to sleep.

Think of how many hours exist between Friday night and Sunday evening. You've got 32 waking hours where you can work on your craft. Do it while everyone else is fooling around and wasting time. If I wanted to be an NFL quarterback or a player in the NBA I know I physically couldn't do it. But comedy is something anybody can do. The only thing separating me and you is 1,000 performances. You can get five minutes together, go and perform, stick with it, persevere. It's something that pretty much anyone can do and so the people that are going to make it are the ones that work hard while everyone else is screwing around.

There are an infinite number of ways to get your stand-up career started. No two people have the same story, and the beauty of stand-up comedy is how you tell those stories in individual ways. Stand-up can be a gateway to other careers in comedy or perhaps a full-time job. It's up to you. No matter what direction you choose to take your stand-up career, you *must* stand up (pun intended) to the challenge that is building your own brand. Successful stand-up comedians run their own businesses. They market themselves. They are resourceful.

Every day people gather together. Whether it's a corporate meeting, a sweet sixteen party, a cruise ship, or a school. Each of these gatherings is an opportunity to perform and practice. The best way to be successful is to keep your eye out for these opportunities. And along your way, remember to write down the humorous moments.

<instructions>Supplemental Materials:

Dan as the voice of Bill Clinton on the radio: http://www.danielnainan.com/index.php?option=com_content&view=article&id=140&Itemid=493

Dan's YouTube video with over 1.1 million views: http://www.youtube.com/watch?v=say9MsdpGXs

Dan on Ted Talks:

http://tedxtalks.ted.com/video/TEDxGlastonbury-Dan-Nainan-Come

Dan does Barack Obama:

http://www.youtube.com/watch?v=sAgv8YXNjkQ&feature=related

Dan does Apple Computer Commercial:

http://www.youtube.com/watch?v=7GIn0hOl05E&feature=related

Keyword	Global Monthly Searches	Notes
stand up comedian	301000	
best stand up comedians	22200	
how to become a standup comedian	1300	
how to be a comedian	9140000	
famous stand up comedians	1300	
female stand up comedians	2900	distinction between female and male comedians evident in first google page search
becoming a stand up comedian	1000	
comedy shows	301000	
comedy show	368000	
stand up comedian tours	260	
comedy central comedians	18100	

hbo stand up comedians	320
hire a stand up comedian	170
how to do stand up comedy	2400
comedy school	49500
aziz ansari stand up	8100
clean stand up comedians	170
stand up comedy jokes	2400
comedians for hire	3600
writing stand up comedy	1000
robin williams standup	5400
ricky gervais standup	5400
daniel tosh standup	9900
tracy morgan standup	2900
standup for kids	6600
stand up videos	14800
celebrity standups	1300
stand up jokes	5400
stand up comedy class	1900
stand up comedy training	210
comedy courses	8100
comedy college	12100
comedy workshops	1900
comedy clubs	823000
improv classes	14800

stand up comedy clinic	36
stand up comedy writing	1000
chicago stand up comedy	1300
comedy acts	12100
free comedy	165000
college comedy	12100
stand up comedy how to	246000
live comedy shows	2400
comedy events	9900
comedy theater	90500

agents and managers

Intro:

definition:http://en.wikipedia.org/wiki/Stand-up_comedy

http://en.wikipedia.org/wiki/Comedian

(History of Stand Up) older/traditional comedy:http://en.wikipedia.org/wiki/Slapstick

http://en.wikipedia.org/wiki/Comedy_genres

How-To Guides:

- http://www.topcomedysecrets.com/
- http://comedians.about.com/od/breakingin/How_to_Break_In_to_Standup_Comedy.htm
- http://www.soyouwanna.com/soyouwanna-stand-up-comedy-1022.html
- askmen.com: http://www.askmen.com/money/how_to_150/184_how_to.html (note – gender roles/differences)
- http://www.essortment.com/become-stand-up-comic-35553.html
- http://www.ehow.com/how_5110969_become-good-standup-comedian.html
- http://www.fabjob.com/Comic.asp

Google Ads:

www.stand-upcomedy.com/LiveYourDream

www.lastandups.com

www.acmecomedy.com

YouTube channels (compile from list): http://en.wikipedia.org/wiki/List_of_stand-up_comedians

(add – newer comedians just breaking in – Megan Amram/people who got famous through Twitter, etc)

General Comedy Sites:

http://www.comedycentral.com/

http://comedians.jokes.com/

http://www.rooftopcomedy.com/

http://www.splashlife.com/article/30-under-30-comedians-watch

splitsider.com

funnyordie.com

</instructions>

Author Fun FAQ

What inspired you to become a standup comedian?

I was a senior engineer with Intel Corporation. My job was to travel with chairman and co-founder Andy Grove, doing technical demonstrations on stage at events all over the world. I was terribly nervous about speaking on stage, so I decided to take a comedy class to get over the fear of public speaking.

What is your favorite food?

I love eating everything – and since I travel all over the world, I get the sample all different kinds of foods. I like to say I've never had a bad meal in my life. If I absolutely had to choose a favorite, I would say steak and lobster.

What is your strangest hobby?

I guess you could say my strangest hobby is something which I avoid doing, and that is watching television. A friend of mine, author Steve Chandler, says that when you're watching television, you're watching other people do what they love doing for living (all the while getting paid lots of money for doing so). He asks, which side of the glass do you want to be on, the side of the few who are doing what they love and getting paid, or the millions who sit and watch passively? I agree 100 percent.

As you might expect, not watching television for 30 hours a week like your typical American enables me to engage in many other hobbies – I play five instruments, love learning languages and I read the New York Times every day, pretty much cover to cover.

What is your favorite quote and why?

My favorite quote is "Do what you fear, and the death of fear is certain." I absolutely love this quote, because it kind of defines how I live my life. I was afraid of water, so I took scuba diving lessons. I was afraid of heights, so I bungee jumped and skydived. I was terrified of speaking on stage, so I took a comedy class. I think it's really important to conquer your fears head-on.

What did you want to be when you were growing up?

I wanted to be one of two things – a pilot, or an entertainer. I'm kind of bummed out that I didn't become a pilot, but it's a lot easier to get a pilot's license once you're an entertainer than to try to be an entertainer once you're a pilot, so maybe I made the right move.

Like then Share!

Click to share a free copy with your Facebook friends

(Don't worry, it won't auto share!)

About The Author

 **Dan Nainan**

Dan Nainan got his start by taking a comedy class to get over the nervousness of speaking on stage. In his job as a demo engineer with Intel Corporation, Dan toured the world with CEO Andy Grove, demonstrating the latest technology for audiences numbering into the thousands.

After leaving Intel to pursue comedy full time, Dan has toured as a feature act with Robert Schimmel and Russell Peters. Dan has appeared on network television including "Last Comic Standing" as well as in feature films, on radio and in an Apple "Get a Mac" commercial, and he performed for Donald Trump in Palm Beach, Florida.

He has performed at TED India, at a Toastmasters International convention, and he recently performed on the Muscular Dystrophy Association Labor Day Telethon live from Las Vegas.

Note to readers:

This eBook is a how-to guide for breaking into the world of stand-up comedy. Co-authored by stand-up comedian, Dan Nainan, and stand-up journalist, Grace DeVoll, the eBook features first-person recollections from Dan's career in the comedy industry. Dan's anecdotes are marked in italics at the beginning of each chapter. The remainder of the eBook contains expert narrative on methods and practices that anyone can use to start off their stand-up comedy career.

About The Publisher

Hyperink is the easiest way for anyone to publish a beautiful, high-quality book.

We work closely with subject matter experts to create each book. We cover topics ranging from higher education to job recruiting, from Android apps marketing to barefoot running.

If you have interesting knowledge that people are willing to pay for, especially if you've already produced content on the topic, please reach out to us! There's no writing required and it's a unique opportunity to build your own brand and earn royalties.

Hyperink is based in SF and actively hiring people who want to shape publishing's future. Email us if you'd like to meet our team!

Note: If you're reading this book in print or on a device that's not web-enabled, **please email** books@hyperinkpress.com with the title of this book in the subject line. We'll send you a PDF copy, so you can access all of the great content we've included as clickable links.

READERS WHO ENJOYED THIS BOOK ALSO ENJOYED!

The Best Book On Goldman Sachs Banking

Want to land an investment banking job at Goldman Sachs? In The Best Book On Goldman Sachs Banking, a Goldman veteran teaches you how to secure your dream job.

$7.99

BUY NOW

The Best Book On Getting An IBanking Internship

Applying to Goldman Sachs, Morgan Stanley, and JPMorgan? A bulge-bracket intern shares her advice on how you can break into investment banking! This ebook covers everything from resumes to interviews to firm cultures.

$25

BUY NOW

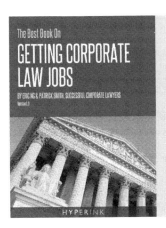

The Best Book On Getting Corporate Law Jobs

Want to learn the exact steps to getting a prestigious corporate law job? Interested in working for Davis Polk, Wilson Sonsini, and other top firms? Hear directly from the students that got in!

$7.99

BUY NOW

Made in the USA
Lexington, KY
27 May 2014